CW01429648

Ian Botham

Andrew Langley

Illustrated by
Karen Heywood

Hamish Hamilton
London

Titles in the Profiles *series*

Ian Botham	0-241-12293-7	Nelson Mandela	0-241-11913-8
Edith Cavell	0-241-11479-9	Bob Marley	0-241-11476-4
Marie Curie	0-241-11741-0	The Queen Mother	0-241-11030-0
Roald Dahl	0-241-11043-2	Florence Nightingale	0-241-11477-2
Thomas Edison	0-241-10713-X	Emmeline Pankhurst	0-241-11478-0
Anne Frank	0-241-11294-X	Anna Pavlova	0-241-10481-5
Elizabeth Fry	0-241-12084-5	Prince Philip	0-241-11167-6
Gandhi	0-241-11166-8	Beatrix Potter	0-241-12051-9
Indira Gandhi	0-241-11772-0	Viv Richards	0-241-12046-2
Amy Johnson	0-241-12317-8	Barry Sheene	0-241-10851-9
Helen Keller	0-241-11295-8	Mother Teresa	0-241-10933-7
John F. Kennedy	0-241-12288-0	Queen Victoria	0-241-10480-7
John Lennon	0-241-11561-2	The Princess of Wales	0-241-11740-2
Martin Luther King	0-241-10931-0		

The artist and publisher would like
to acknowledge Patrick Eagar for his kind permission
to use his photographs as reference.

HAMISH HAMILTON CHILDREN'S BOOKS

Published by the Penguin Group
27 Wrights Lane, London W8 5TZ, England
Viking Penguin Inc., 40 West 23rd Street, New York, New York 10010, U.S.A.
Penguin Books Australia Ltd, Ringwood, Victoria, Australia
Penguin Books Canada Ltd, 2801 John Street, Markham, Ontario, Canada L3R 1B4
Penguin Books (N.Z.) Ltd, 182–190 Wairau Road, Auckland 10, New Zealand

Penguin Books Ltd, Registered Offices: Harmondsworth, Middlesex, England

First published in Great Britain 1988 by
Hamish Hamilton Children's Books

Text copyright © 1988 by Andrew Langley
Illustrations copyright © 1988 by Karen Heywood

British Library Cataloguing in Publication Data
Langley, Andrew
Ian Botham.—2nd ed.—(Profiles).
1. Botham, Ian   2. Cricket players—
England—Biography—Juvenile literature
I. Title   II. Heywood, Karen   III. Series
796.35'0924   GV915.B5/
ISBN 0-241-12293-7

Typeset by Pioneer
Printed in Great Britain at the
University Press, Cambridge

Contents

Ian Botham

1 The Boy Wonder

Ian Botham is the sort of cricketer every schoolboy dreams of becoming. He hits huge sixes into the crowd when he is batting, sends the stumps flying when he is bowling, and picks up brilliant catches when he is fielding. Over the years, he has never been too worried by failure or defeat, and has inspired his team-mates with his endless self-confidence.

Out on the cricket field, he is always on the attack. He still believes that he can beat any opponent, and has a simple motto: 'when I am batting the bowler isn't good enough, and when I am bowling the batsman isn't good enough.' But he is also a sporting player who, however hard he tries on the field, is the best of friends with his opponents at the end of the day.

Ian Botham was born on 24 November 1955 in Heswall, a small town on the Wirral peninsula in Cheshire. His father and mother were living there for a short time before moving across the Irish Sea to Londonderry in Northern Ireland. Ian's father was a Chief Petty Officer in the Fleet Air Arm at that time, and a skilled aircraft engineer.

Ian was the eldest child in the family. He very soon grew to be big for his age, and was very competitive.

Even at the age of two, he took part in a toddlers' race and won by knocking over all the other children! Not long after this, his father retired from the Navy and went to work for a helicopter company in Yeovil. This Somerset town was to be Ian's home for the next thirteen years. It was a fine centre for sport, with a county cricket ground and a Southern League football team. Taunton, the headquarters of Somerset's cricket side, was only a few kilometres away.

The sporting influence on the young Botham was very strong. His father had played cricket, hockey and football regularly wherever he was stationed with the Fleet Air Arm. When he settled in Yeovil, he still turned out for the firm's cricket team every Saturday in

Ian with his sisters and cousins when he was 8

the summer. Botham's mother had also been a notable cricketer during her time as a nurse in the Second World War, and had been captain of her detachment's team.

The Bothams' house was right next to the sports ground belonging to the local grammar school, and it wasn't long before Ian was scrambling through the hedge and watching the boys in the cricket nets. He became such a regular spectator that the games master soon allowed him to fetch balls that had been hit out of the nets. Eventually, he even joined in with the coaching sessions, which gave him his first taste of the game.

Cricket quickly became one of the most important things in his life. After watching the grammar school boys over the hedge, he would practise hard at what he had seen. From the very start, he was given a great deal of help and encouragement by his father. The pair would go off together on Saturday afternoons to the grounds where Botham senior was playing. Young Ian would always bring his kit just in case the side was one short, and often got a game.

He played cricket whenever and wherever he could. It became a common sight to see him hanging around the Mudford Road Recreation Ground, cricket gear at the ready, hoping for a game — and he was barely nine years old. He was big and strong for his age, and easily made his way into the cricket and football teams at his Junior School. Most of his team-mates were two years older, but he was already the star, scoring goals and hitting massive sixes.

At this early stage in his sporting life, he was lucky to be coached by a games master, Richard Hibbitt, who did not try to stifle his natural aggression. Mr Hibbitt encouraged him to hit the ball hard, bowl a good line and length, and not to worry too much about a correct 'style'. Botham has always been grateful for this, and has never taken too much notice of cricket textbooks since. He was able to develop his own style of playing, once he had got the basics right.

At the age of thirteen, he went on to Buckler's Mead Secondary School in Yeovil, where his size and sporting talents were soon spotted. Among those who noticed him was Bill Andrews, a fine fast bowler for Somerset in his day, and someone who kept an eagle eye on good young cricketers in the county. That summer, Botham was picked for the Somerset Under-15 team to play against Wiltshire. He was an instant success, hitting his side out of trouble with a furious innings.

In fact, he was a success in nearly every sport he took up. He was captain of the school's football team, and a county badminton champion. When he turned fifteen, he was registered by Bill Andrews for Somerset County Cricket Club. He had no doubt at all about his ability to hit a bowler for six, or score a winning goal.

This kind of confidence amazed the other boys he played with. Among these were Phil Slocombe, Vic Marks and Peter Roebuck, who were all to join him later in the Somerset First XI. Botham's determination to succeed was unusual for such a youngster, but in spite of his big frame and his strength, he did not seem to be a Test star in the making. Occasionally, he would put on a whirlwind performance — once scoring 83 out of a stand of 95 with Roebuck — but he was not consistent enough.

Even if his cricket colleagues couldn't see how hugely talented the fifteen-year-old Botham was, there were plenty of others who could. Not long after he was registered with Somerset as a cricketer, he was thrilled to receive an offer to become a professional footballer from Bert Head, the manager of First Division Crystal Palace.

In those days, only a few years after England's World Cup win, football was more popular than it had ever been. An established professional with a big club side would be paid a handsome wage. Cricket, on the other hand, had lost some of its glamour, and the Somerset team was struggling. A county cricket professional was not at all well paid, and had no guarantee of a job during the winter.

Professional footballer or professional cricketer — it was a hard choice for Botham to make, and he spent a lot of time discussing it with his father. In the end, he chose cricket. The main reason for this was his deep love for the game: 'I want to be always playing it and I love talking about it,' he says. 'More than anything cricket is fun. I enjoy every second that I am on the field.'

2 Playing for Somerset

As soon as he left school at the age of seventeen, Botham
was invited to join the ground staff at Lord's in London
— 'headquarters' of cricket and MCC (Marylebone
Cricket Club). This was a wonderful opportunity to
learn about the skills of cricket at the best coaching
school in the country. The ground staff consisted of
promising young players from all parts of England,
who spent two years finding out about first-class cricket
from the very bottom. They had to sell score-cards at
the ground, sweep up, run errands for the senior
players and help the groundsman with his work, as
well as playing matches themselves, and spending time
in the nets.

Ian was still a member of the Somerset staff as well,
and most weekends he would travel back home to play
in a Second XI game. His appetite for cricket grew
bigger, and he would spend every spare day he could
in the nets, improving his batting and his bowling.

When Botham joined the Lord's ground staff, his
father had given him two things to aim for: 'play for
your county at eighteen, and your country before
twenty-five.' In fact, he got into the Somerset team two
months before his eighteenth birthday. He had been

having an up-and-down season for the Second XI, with a top score of 82 but only 9 wickets in the bag. When he heard that he had been selected for the Sunday League game against Sussex, he was thrilled — partly because he had reached the senior team before colleagues like Roebuck and Slocombe.

The Somerset team was led by Brian Close, a tough Yorkshireman who was feared by most of the team. He only allowed Botham to bowl three overs, which were hit for 22 runs, but the young man redeemed himself by taking a fine catch in the outfield. The following Sunday he played again, and took his very first wicket for Somerset, getting New Zealander Geoff Howarth leg-before-wicket. His career had begun.

*

Somerset was still one of the poor relations among the first-class counties. The team had never won the Championship or any of the one-day titles, and few of its players had reached the Test arena. However, 1974 saw a remarkable number of talented young cricketers challenging for places in the team. As well as Botham, there was a highly entertaining batsman from Antigua in the West Indies, Viv Richards. It was clear that Richards was an exceptional cricketer, fast in his reactions and savage in his hitting of the ball. Botham recognises the best when he sees it, and he and Richards soon became firm friends and rivals.

Botham played in his first county match in the May of that year, against Lancashire at Taunton. Bristling with aggression, and showing no sign of nerves at this important point in his career, he slammed three boundaries before being caught off a weak shot in the covers for 13. He trudged back angrily to the pavilion — annoyed not because he had put the ball into the air, but because he hadn't hit it harder!

His first wicket came at last in a game against Gloucestershire, but he had not really done enough to impress the stern Close, and he was dropped to the Second XI. This setback made him angry rather than sad, and he worked hard at improving his technique both in batting and in bowling. All this time his mate Viv Richards was racing away towards his first thousand runs in a season, and delighting crowds with his glorious batting. By June, Richards already had two centuries under his belt, and a string of fifties.

On the morning of 12 June, Botham had resigned himself to missing out on another big occasion — the quarter-final match against Hampshire in the Benson and Hedges competition. Then, less than an hour before play began at Taunton, Brian Close told him that he would be taking the place of Allan Jones. This was the chance he had been looking for, against a side with two of the world's best players in it: the South African batsman Barry Richards and the West Indian fast bowler Andy Roberts.

Hampshire batted first, and Botham got into the action early. Coming on as first-change seamer, he bowled the great Barry Richards. His eleven overs were much more accurate than the wayward ones of earlier limited-overs games, and he finished with a tidy

2 for 33. Somerset were left to get 183 to win and go through to the semi-finals.

When Botham walked out to the wicket, the score was 113 for 7, and the target seemed a long way away. But, as Jim Parks passed him, he said, 'It's still on, just keep your head.' The encouragement steadied his nerves, though seam bowler Tom Cartwright was caught off the very next ball to make it 113 for 8. The next batsman was Hallam Moseley, and Botham went up to him to decide what to do. They were determined to play sensibly and not throw away their wickets.

Sure enough, with Moseley pushing singles, and his partner hitting a boundary now and then, the score steadily mounted. Roberts was brought back on to try and finish the game with his speed, and with Somerset still needing 31 runs to win he bowled a fierce bouncer at Botham which hit him in the face. Botham fell to the ground with blood trickling from his mouth and two of his teeth broken.

In spite of his injury, he refused to go off the field. The blow from Roberts was like a challenge to him, and a character like Botham was not going to back down from it. He smacked the next ball for three, and now he knew deep down that Somerset were going to win. Moseley was out with only 7 runs needed, but the last batsman hung on until Botham drove a ball from Herman through the covers to the boundary, and they were there.

Botham, with 45 not out, was named Man of the Match. More than that, he was a new Somerset hero, a man who hit sixes, fielded brilliantly and fought hard

Botham is consoled after he has been struck in the mouth

in a crisis. His name appeared in newspaper headlines up and down the country, and for the first time he knew what it was to be famous.

He finished the season with more than 400 runs and 30 wickets to his credit, and his promising start was noticed by a writer in *Wisden's Almanack*. His performances showed 'star quality', said the writer, who went on to praise Botham's 'lively right-arm swing bowling, clean flowing driving and brilliant fielding.'

3 A Local Hero

By the summer of 1974, Ian Botham had come a long way in a short time. He had become a regular member of the Somerset side, and had been marked down as a star of the future — all at the age of eighteen. On top of that, he had met the girl who was later to become his wife, Kathryn Waller. She was also the god-daughter of Brian Close, and the fearsome Somerset captain was none too happy about her marrying a tearaway like Botham.

Nevertheless, the couple got engaged that Christmas. Kathryn knew what she was taking on, and that her future husband would be away from her for long periods in the summer. Botham was to write later: 'the family life of a cricketer in England is not much to write home about.' When eventually they bought a house in the village of Epworth in Lincolnshire, he found that he rarely got home at all during the season. The only time he could see Kathryn and later his children was when they came to stay at the team's hotel.

The life of a county cricketer became a lot more complicated during the 1970s. There were fewer three-day matches, and the spaces were filled with new one-day competitions. Sundays were taken up with the John

Kathryn Botham with baby Sarah

Player League, so that very often teams could find themselves playing cricket every day for several weeks. To cap it all, they would often have to travel from one end of the country to the other in between matches. The Bothams' decision to live so far away from Somerset added to their difficulties.

Botham expected a lot of himself in the 1975 season, but was disappointed. He played in twenty matches, and bowled more overs than anyone else. Cartwright, playing out his last summer with Somerset, helped with some expert coaching of Ian's bowling. The teaching of such an experienced man was still valuable to Botham, but he was never going to be a nagging line-and-length bowler. His speed was increasing, and he was always trying something new; this often led to wild and expensive spells of bowling.

His batting was even more wayward, as the season's average of just over 17 showed. He was still trying to hit the cover off the ball, and looking at times just like a slogger. But shrewd observers could see that there was a highly gifted batsman in the making, as he revealed in the occasional magnificent stroke.

As a Somerset staff member, he was paid a wage only during the cricket season, and had to find another job in the winter. One year he worked on a building site in Yeovil to build up his muscles. The next he became a travelling salesman, selling drums and drumsticks all over the country. Every Saturday he played football as centre forward in the Somerset Senior League.

1976 opened on a high note, when Ian and Kathryn were married and moved up to live in their Lincolnshire farmhouse. The year continued happily for Botham, and at the beginning of the new season he was given his county cap by Brian Close. For this summer at least, he wouldn't have to worry about being overshadowed by Viv Richards, who was touring England with the West Indies team.

His batting improved in leaps and bounds, and he showed that he was willing to buckle down and play longer innings. In May, he came agonisingly close to his maiden century when he hit 97 against Sussex, and made an impressive fifty against the West Indies tourists. Close signalled his approval by moving Botham to Number 4 in the order.

The result was electrifying. Against Nottinghamshire, he scored 80 in the first innings, and Somerset were set 301 to win. Botham came in with the score at 51 for 2 and proceeded to pull his first ball for a six. He carried on in much the same way, scoring 167 of the runs his side needed, and sweeping them to an extraordinary victory. His not-out innings contained six sixes and twenty fours.

He opened the Somerset bowling regularly as well, and grabbed his chance with some devastating performances. The most remarkable of these was the 6 for 16 he took to demolish Hampshire, Barry Richards and all. He also took 11 wickets in a match against Gloucestershire, by far the best figures in his short career.

These flamboyant deeds caught the eye of the England selectors, who were desperately searching for new talent after a summer in which their Test team had been hammered into the ground by the mighty West Indians. Botham was picked for two of the Prudential Trophy matches at the end of the season but, against such powerful opponents, he looked a little raw. At Scarborough, his three overs cost 26 runs, and at Edgbaston his next three cost 31 runs. Playing at this level was clearly a far cry from the county game.

He knew now that he could not be too far away from the full Test side, although he was not chosen for the winter tour of India. Instead, he spent the winter in

Australia on a Whitbread cricket scholarship. As it was a rainy year, he did not get much cricket in, but hit the headlines when he met Ian Chappell, the outspoken Australian captain, in a bar in Melbourne. It was rumoured that Chappell began to make rude remarks about the quality of English cricket, and Botham, after warning him once, punched him off his bar stool and onto the floor.

Whether this is true or not, Botham does have a lot of natural aggression and strength. On occasion, these can explode with frustration if they are not used up on the cricket field. Botham's fellow cricketers know only too well how quickly he becomes bored in the dressing room if there is nothing going on. He prowls around like a caged tiger, looking for some way of stirring up excitement with a practical joke or an argument. Fast bowler Bob Willis says with a smile, 'I honestly think Ian would like to have a friendly punch-up with someone once a week, just to relieve his pent-up aggression.'

By great good luck, Botham was in Melbourne at the same time as the England team arrived to play the Centenary Test Match with Australia. It was a grand occasion, with many celebrations and speeches, and a host of famous cricketers present. Without turning a hair, Botham mingled with the England party and tagged along with them to parties and receptions. Many people thought he was actually a member of the team!

4 Into the England Team

Botham was to see quite a lot of the Australian touring team during 1977. In May he was at Bath where, in glorious sunshine, Somerset beat the tourists for the first time in their history. Botham's own contribution was impressive: 4 wickets in the second innings, a fierce 59 (with three sixes) and 39 not out, including the winning stroke.

The England selectors could hardly ignore this, and Botham was picked for the MCC match against the Australians the following week. This was a kind of Test trial, but the twenty-one-year-old did not come out of it too well. He tried to bowl too fast and was hit all round the ground. However, he was not written off, and was named as twelfth man during the series of one-day internationals.

He was not in the teams for the first two Tests, and in fact there was no obvious place for him. Tony Greig was the team's all-rounder, and there were plenty of other seam bowlers in the side. Then, in July, Chris Old was injured and forced to drop out, and Botham heard over the radio that he had been picked as the replacement.

One of Botham's greatest assets has been his confidence in himself. When he arrived in the Trent Bridge dressing room, he was not at all overawed by the presence of stars like Geoff Boycott, Alan Knott or Derek Underwood, all of whom had been playing Test cricket for more than ten years. They were surprised when he butted in on their conversations and gave his opinions without any shyness.

He was glad that England fielded first, for that meant that he wouldn't have to wait about in the dressing room. He was soon in action as first-change bowler, but was wayward in his line, sending too many deliveries down the leg side, and Brearley took him off.

But it wasn't long before he made his mark, taking an easy catch off the bowling of Underwood. When he came on for his second spell, the match was finely balanced at 131 for 2. At the other end was Greg Chappell, Australia's captain and one of the very best attacking batsmen in the world. The first ball of the over was dreadful — a long hop outside the off-stump — and Chappell pounced on it eagerly, only to edge it into his stumps. Once again, Botham's luck had held: it's not surprising that his team-mates were soon calling him 'Golden Arm', for his habit of picking up good wickets with bad balls.

With his first Test wicket under his belt, Botham's bowling improved dramatically. He dismissed Walters and Marsh in one over, and by the end of the day had taken 5 for 74. Australia were all out for 243, and England won the match comfortably, by 7 wickets.

In the Fourth Test at Leeds, he bowled even better. Together with the naggingly accurate Mike Hendrick, he destroyed the Australian first innings, taking 5 for 21 as they plunged to 103 all out and an eventual innings defeat. The conditions were perfect for him, with clouds overhead, and his deliveries swung devastatingly late.

His glory was short-lived this time, however. Because he had had a lot of success when wearing a particular pair of cricket boots, he came to believe that they were his 'lucky charm', and wore them, as he says 'long after they should have gone in the dustbin.' The result was that he strained his left foot badly. When, on the fourth day of the match, he trod on the ball by mistake, he fractured a bone in his foot.

That was the end of the series for him. His foot was put in plaster, and he missed the final Test at the Oval, as well as several county games. Since then he has made sure that all his equipment is in good condition, and doesn't hang onto a pair of boots that are past their prime!

But there were plenty of compensations. His son Liam was born in the August of that year, and he and Kathryn took a well-deserved holiday. He was chosen as one of the England party to tour Pakistan and New Zealand, and the Cricket Writers' Club voted him the Young Cricketer of the Year. Buyers of *Wisden's Almanack* discovered that he had also been chosen as one of the five Cricketers of the Year.

By that time, Botham was sweating in the heat of Pakistan: not on the cricket pitch, but on the golf course, for he had very few innings on the tour. When the party arrived in New Zealand, however, he was in his

Ian with Paul Downton and Mike Brearley. Ian has just been awarded the prize for best under-25 all rounder.

element again. He forced his way back into the Test side with a century in the first provincial game, and bowled better on the greener and more helpful pitches.

The First Test was a disaster for England. With Geoff Boycott leading the side in place of the injured Brearley, some of the team spirit seemed to disappear. Set to score 137 to win, they were shot out for 64, and New Zealand had won her first-ever victory over the Old Country.

Things seemed to be going no better for the tourists in the Second Test when Botham walked to the crease with the score at 128 for 5. In an unusually disciplined innings, he stayed there for more than five hours, scoring 103 — his first Test century.

England gained a big lead and, when they went in to bat again, wanted quick runs to be able to force a victory. Unfortunately, one of the men batting was Boycott, who found it even more difficult than usual to push the run-rate along. Back in the dressing-room, a quick vote was taken, and Botham was delegated to do something about the snail's pace. His solution was to run Boycott out — on purpose. The Yorkshireman was enraged, and was heard to mutter, 'That's what you get when you're playing with schoolboys!'

Throughout the series, Botham was having a more than schoolboyish battle with the New Zealand fast bowler Richard Hadlee. Always eager to rise to a challenge, he had tried to hook Hadlee's searing bouncers as often as possible. In turn, he bowled bouncers at Hadlee, who had to admit: 'when Botham started to bowl at my head, my confidence went.' Botham had won that round.

Indeed, he had established himself firmly in the England team. He took over the job of all-rounder from Tony Greig, and added some dash and vigour to what was a rather dull batting line-up. Above all, he had the sort of swashbuckling self-assurance which inspired those around him.

5 Botham the Superstar

1978 was the year in which Ian Botham became a household name. Against what was admittedly weak opposition, he piled up runs and wickets with his own exciting brand of aggression. In a damp and chilly summer, he brought the crowds flocking to Test Matches just to see him play.

The Pakistani team arrived that summer for a Test series. Botham scored two centuries against them in a row, both of them murderous efforts against a wilting attack. At least, it wilted when Botham came to the crease. In the Second Test at Lord's, England were tottering on 134 for 5 when he joined Graham Roope at the wicket. It was a dull and damp day, and the Pakistan bowlers were making the most of the conditions.

This was Botham's first Test at Lord's, the head-quarters of the game, and he was determined to make it a spectacular occasion. True to form, he pulled his second ball for a huge six into the Mound Stand, and by tea had scored 24 not out. After tea he scored even faster as he tried to reach his century before the end of play. At one point he drove a ball straight back at Liaquat Ali so fiercely that the bowler flung himself to the ground rather than try and catch it!

The century came up in the last over with a cover drive for four, and the crowd, which had grown quickly since tea, went home very happy. But that wasn't the end of Botham's destruction of the touring side. The following Monday, he took 8 wickets for 34 to skittle them out for 139 in their second innings.

Bowling against Pakistan

In the second half of the summer, there were three more Tests against New Zealand. Botham did little with the bat, but more than made up for it by taking 24 wickets — at a rate of 8 per game!

The news that he was in the party to tour Australia that winter cannot really have come as a surprise. He made the most of the short break in the autumn to spend time with his wife (who was expecting their second baby, Sarah) and son in Epworth, go out shooting with his friends, and watch the local football side, struggling Scunthorpe United.

He needed a good rest, but it's difficult for Ian Botham to stay out of the headlines for long. At a farewell party in the local pub, he accidentally put his left arm through a glass doorway and cut his wrist badly. In fact, it might have finished his career for good, but luckily there was no damage to the nerve. The wrist was quickly stitched and bandaged, and he was fit enough to fly out with the rest of the party in November.

The tour of Australia was a gruelling one, with six Test matches to be played. Botham had to work hard for runs and wickets in the heat of the Australian summer. Without ever really taking charge, he made several vital contributions to the team's success, including a thunderous 74 to rescue them from a desperate position in the Fifth Test. After he had put in every ounce of his strength, and the Ashes were safe with England, he longed to get back home and put his feet up.

*

Modern cricket is an almost non-stop business. When Ian Botham got back to his farmhouse in South Humberside, he had played in seventeen Test Matches in just eighteen months — and missed out on four more! On top of that had been games in the County Championship, the John Player League, the Benson and Hedges Cup and the Gillette Cup for Somerset, tour matches, benefit matches and charity games.

Botham's strength and confidence, not to mention his cricketing genius, had carried him through it all, from the gloom of a wet English summer to the broiling heat of an Australian drought.

He had had a rocketing start to his Test career. At the beginning of the 1979 season, he was within sight of a remarkable 'double' — 1000 runs and 100 wickets in Test Matches. Several players had performed the feat before, notably Maurice Tate, Richie Benaud and the great Gary Sobers. The quickest of them at that time was the Indian Vinoo Mankad, who had taken only twenty-three matches to reach the target.

Records don't mean much to Ian Botham. He rarely worries about his batting or bowling averages, preferring to defeat the other side — if possible, single-handed. But he couldn't help getting caught up in the excitement as the series with India drew near.

Botham had little chance of improving his run tally in the First Test against India, for when he came to the wicket, the scoreboard already showed 400 runs. He made a quick 33 and the England total eventually reached a mammoth 633 for 5, with the young David Gower not out on 200.

India subsided to an innings defeat, not surprisingly. Botham himself took three catches and raised his total of Test wickets to 94. In the next Match, at Lord's, he skittled out the Indians again in their first innings to reach a tantalising 99, and had to wait until the following Monday before he could get at them again.

With his parents, wife and children watching from the stands, Botham tried everything he could to reach the magic number. He bowled from close to the stumps to give his outswinger a greater angle; he bowled inswingers; he slipped in the odd bouncer. Then at last, in mid-afternoon, Gavaskar touched a ball to Brearley in the slips and he was there.

The thousand runs took a little longer. He almost got there in the Third Test at Leeds, smashing a brilliant 137 which included 99 runs before lunch. Finally, at the Oval, he square cut Bedi to the boundary and the 'double' was complete. It had taken him only twenty-one matches to achieve — an astounding new record.

Even now, he had little time for rest as the long slog of international cricket carried on. To take his mind off the summer game for a while, Botham took to training with the Scunthorpe United side. Football needed different attitudes and skills. He was running all the time, on or off the ball, and it was a team game with less room for individual brilliance than cricket.

By November he was on board a plane with the England party, heading once more for Australia. Many of the players were unhappy about this tour: they had seen quite enough of the Australian team over the last three years.

They played three Test Matches and lost every one. The only bright spot in the tour was the performance of Botham, who at last showed the Australian public the sort of form that had made him the most exciting young cricketer in the world. At Melbourne he scored his first Test century against Australia, ending not out on 119.

On the way home in February, the England tourists stopped off at Bombay to play a Golden Jubilee Test Match against India. It was supposed to be an Indian celebration, but Botham dominated the match from the first day, when he took 6 wickets. He followed this up with 114 to save England from a bad start, and then wiped out the Indians again to finish with an incredible 13 wickets in the match. As an all-round performance in a single Test Match it has never been equalled.

6 Captain of England

There now seemed to be no limit to what Ian Botham could do on a cricket field. In only twenty-five Test Matches, he had scored 1336 runs and taken 139 wickets. The next step up would have to be the captaincy of England. Mike Brearley did not want to go on tour again, so who was going to take his place? It was clear that the selectors were grooming the twenty-five-year-old for the job. He had led the England team for one match in Australia, and performed well, although he had little experience as a captain. Botham was poised for his biggest test yet.

In 1980, he was named as captain of the England team in the two one-day matches against the West Indian tourists, and it was clear that he would be captain for the Test series as well. He was, at twenty-four, one of the youngest Englishmen ever to lead their country.

While many people were thrilled at the news — especially in Somerset — others were less happy. They felt that he was too young and too much a law unto himself to be an effective captain. On top of that, he had a lot to do on the field already, speeding up the scoring rate with the bat, bowling long spells and fielding in the slips. How could he have the time or the energy to work out team strategy as well?

Exactly a week later, Botham celebrated the news in a grand manner by hitting 228 in three hours against Gloucestershire. It was his first double century, and included a county record of ten sixes, not to mention twenty-seven fours.

Things seemed to be running as well as ever, and the two one-day international matches were just as encouraging. After losing the first game through slow batting, England beat the West Indies in the second. In a thrilling finish, Botham and his Somerset team-mate Vic Marks scored the winning runs, and honours were even.

At this point the going got much tougher. The West Indies XI was easily the strongest team in the world, with a terrifying all-pace attack led by Holding and Roberts, a master batsman in Viv Richards, and an inspiring captain in Clive Lloyd. The England team, on the other hand, was a mixture of players past their best and youngsters who had not yet proved themselves.

But in the first Test, at Nottingham, they nearly pulled off a victory in a low-scoring game. Set to score 208 to win, the West Indies were whittled down to 180 for 7, but still managed to win. The blame for England's losing was put squarely upon the fielding, where several important catches were spilled.

At Lord's, the West Indians showed the immense power of their batting by scoring 518 in the first innings. After that, England scarcely had a chance of a win in the series, and were lucky not to lose another game, helped by rain and some dogged tail-end batting.

The eagerly-awaited Centenary Test Match against the Australians at Lord's was an even greater disappointment. England were outplayed most of the way through, and the crowds were angry at the amount of time lost through rain. The final straw came when Greg Chappell set England the sporting target of 370 to win in 350 minutes. In contrast to his normal attacking instincts, Botham told his batsmen to hold out for a draw, and the great occasion fizzled out in boredom.

In figures, England had lost only one match that season. Much more disturbing, the team seemed to have lost Ian Botham as a dominant cricketer. In ten innings, he had scored only 169 runs, and 14 wickets was way below his usual haul. He had lost some of his happy confidence, too, and with it the good luck that

Being interviewed with West Indies captain, Clive Lloyd

seemed his by right.

Botham was very annoyed by the sneering comments of newspaper reporters. When he was being a roaring success, they praised him to the skies, but now that he was having a bad patch, they turned against him. Apart from criticising his captaincy and his performances, they accused him of being too fat. They even asked his four-year-old son Liam what his daddy ate every day.

They seemed to forget that no other young captain had been faced straightaway with such formidable opposition. After the series at home, Botham led the English touring party out to the West Indies, which would mean ten matches in succession against Lloyd's men — no easy task.

The West Indian tour was just as tough as expected. England had a poor batting side, and, apart from some magnificent performances by Gooch, Gower and Willey, they were torn to shreds on the hard wickets. They lost the First Test by the huge margin of an innings and 79 runs, and the Third by 298 runs. The Second Test was called off after the government of Guyana objected to the inclusion of Robin Jackman in the side (he had coached in South Africa).

A far worse tragedy struck, off the field. Ken Barrington, the team's much-loved assistant manager, died of a heart attack in the middle of the tour. This sad event lowered the spirits of the Englishmen still further.

Botham's run of bad form continued. In the four Test Matches, his highest score was a mere 26, and he took 15 wickets, bowling more overs than any other

Frustration beginning to show as Ian, the captain,
asks the crowd if they want to 'have a go'!

seamer. He was a shadow of his former world-conquering self, and there was a worried look on his face instead of the devil-may-care smile. Yet through his troubles he managed to keep his players and opponents happy, and the atmosphere between the two teams was friendly and relaxed.

7 The Incredible Tests

During the first six months of 1981, Botham had reached the lowest point in his sensational career so far. It was cruelly unfortunate that his first series as captain had been against the West Indies, who were not only the finest side in the world at that time, but also one of the most fearsome in the history of cricket.

It seemed that England might have a slightly easier task against the touring Australians that summer. After all, the great fast bowler Dennis Lillee was past his prime, and the brilliant Greg Chappell had stayed at home. Instead of having to duck and weave against a barrage of bouncers, they would be facing an attack that was mainly medium pace.

That was Botham's hope, but after the First Test at Nottingham his heart was right down in his boots again. England were bowled out cheaply in both innings, and dropped half-a-dozen important catches as Australia made the better use of a poor pitch. The England captain did little to redeem himself with bat or ball. In fact he had lost so much confidence in himself that he bowled only 26 overs in the match.

It is hardly surprising that the pressure on him was getting too much. He told Dennis Lillee that he had expected to be dropped, not just as captain, but as a player, after this defeat. The newspapers jeeringly called for his resignation, and one television programme was turned into a cruel 'Trial of Ian Botham', which upset him greatly. Kathryn, too, could hardly leave the house without being pestered by reporters.

Botham admits that he went through the Second Test Match at Lord's in a daze. It was a dreary draw, ruined by rain, and the most exciting moment came when angry spectators started to throw cushions onto the pitch! Botham himself had a miserable time, being out for nought in each innings, the first time he had ever collected a 'pair' in a Test. For the first time, also, there was not even a smattering of sympathetic applause as

Leaving the West Indies

41

he trudged back to the pavilion.

His resignation from the captaincy came as no surprise. The worries of leading the side had obviously affected his play, although he was the last to admit it. He had not scored a century or taken five wickets in an innings since the Jubilee Test against India, fourteen long months before.

Mike Brearley was recalled to take on the job. He was the man to get the best out of Botham, who had enormous respect for his shrewd cricketing brain. Brearley had never lost a Test series in England, but with his side one-nil down and four matches still to play, he had a tough task before him.

One of the first things Brearley did on returning to the Test scene was to begin building up Botham's confidence again. This wasn't just a matter of encouraging him — Brearley knew that he hated being given orders. So he teased him as well, asking him if he wanted to be left out of the Test side, and calling him 'The Sidestep Queen' because of his crooked new way of running in to bowl.

This treatment sparked off all Botham's old attacking instincts again. In the Australian first innings in the Third Test at Leeds, he was the best of the English bowlers, with 6 wickets for 95. He was top scorer in England's first innings with 50.

In spite of his efforts, England looked certain to suffer a crushing defeat, and with it the loss of the Ashes. They were forced to follow on their first innings and crumbled to 135 for 7, still more than 90 runs behind. At this point, with most of the crowd having gone home in disappointment, Botham was joined at the wicket by Graham Dilley.

There now followed one of the most rousing partnerships in all cricket. Taking their luck in their hands, the pair began to hammer the tiring Australian pace bowlers all over the field. Swinging through the line, they missed a lot, but hit a lot as well — very hard. In eighty minutes, they added 117 runs. When Dilley was out, Chris Old gave support as Botham raced to his century off only 87 balls.

He ended not out with 149, his highest Test score at that time. His heroic effort had suddenly brought the series alive again, and the whole England team was inspired by it. The Australians still needed only 130 runs to win, however. Botham again struck the first blow: Brearley knew that he would be brimming with confidence, and asked him to open the bowling. In his second over, he had Wood caught behind, and the rest of the Australians were swept aside by Bob Willis.

England won the match by 18 runs, and drew level in the series. The next Test was at Edgbaston, and had an equally incredible climax. As before, the Australians were on the verge of a well-deserved victory: needing 151 to win, they inched their way to 114 for 5. Botham was not too keen to bowl, but Brearley threw him the ball and told him not to give any runs away. In forty minutes, he was hit for just one run, and took the last 5 wickets as well!

The Australians, and the British public, could hardly believe their eyes. After more than a year of lacklustre performances, England had gained two sensational

Alderman is bowled by Botham in the 4th Test against
Australia at Edgbaston

victories in succession. Since he had resigned from the
captaincy, Ian Botham had played like a giant refreshed,
and the team had responded joyfully.

But there was another piece of history to be made
that summer. In the Fifth Test at Manchester, England
were batting well until a middle-order collapse reduced
them to 104 for 5. Botham came in and played even
better than he had at Leeds. This time there were few
mistakes and a range of classical shots, including three
sixes off Lillee in two overs. His 118 was one of the
great innings of modern Test Cricket.

This superb century put the match out of Australia's reach, and England won to go 3-1 up in the series. The final Test at the Oval was a draw, but Botham still made his mark by taking 10 wickets. In four games since Lord's he had scored 365 runs, taken 28 wickets and held 9 catches. No player before him — not the great Dr W. G. Grace, not the run-machine Don Bradman, not even the glorious all-rounder Gary Sobers — had had such a decisive effect on a Test series.

8   Triumphs and Disappointments

Ian Botham flew off to India with the England team
that winter in high spirits. It was his first full tour of
the sub-continent, but all his memories were pleasant
ones — 13 wickets and 114 runs in the Jubilee Test two
years earlier.

As it turned out, Botham was the most consistent of
the Englishmen in the Test Matches, topping the
batting averages and taking more wickets than anyone
else. But it was not a happy tour. After India won the
First Test in Bombay, they were determined that their
opponents should have no chance of levelling the series.
The result was five very dull draws in succession — the
pitches were dead, the action slow, and the England
team frustrated.

On the credit side, however, was a new-style Ian
Botham. In the First Test, he had tried to hammer
England out of trouble, as he had done against the
Australians. After hitting a six, he was caught in the
deep. In the next Test, he took on a much more
responsible role, curbing his impulse to take a swing at
the spinners on the deceptively slow pitch.

England were in a poor position at 230 for 6 when
Botham arrived to join Mike Gatting. In his first forty

minutes at the crease, he scored only 7 runs, without any of his usual dangerous sweeps or lofted drives. Altogether, he made 55: not a big innings by his standards, but one that showed him emerging as a thoughtful, disciplined Test batsman.

This was followed by Test scores of 66, 58, 31, 52 and 142 — a consistency that he had never achieved before. He did it in the face of fine spin-bowling and some disappointing performances by his own side. He even began the Fifth Test with a fever — he had sweated such a lot the night before that Kathryn had had to change his sheets several times.

However, even Indian pitches could not prevent him from giving some enthralling displays of hitting in other matches. The most spectacular of these was against Central Zone, when he blasted a century in only fifty minutes, with seven sixes and sixteen fours. It was his fastest hundred to date, and one of the fastest in cricket history.

The summer of 1982 brought two touring sides to England — India and Pakistan. The home team gained revenge of a sort by beating the Indians one nothing. Botham's maturity as a batsman was shown by his promotion to Number 5 in the order, and he responded by scoring more heavily than ever — 67; 128 and 208.

That double century is his highest Test score so far, and was made off only 225 balls. The power in the shots was typically Botham, and so was the way he got out. Trying to play an extravagant reverse sweep, he was caught easily, entertaining to the last. But that was the end of his big scoring for the season. In the short series

Botham reaches 200 against India (3rd Cornhill Test)

against Pakistan, he was for once overshadowed by another all-rounder, Imran Khan.

Botham's run of bad form continued during the England tour of Australia that winter. Once again, his luck seemed to desert him, for he scored only one fifty during the series and failed to take five wickets in an innings. England lost the Ashes to Australia, and many people blamed Botham for the defeat. This was unfair, because he was still the leading wicket-taker, but his bowling was sometimes off-target and his batting was disappointing.

The truth was that he was tired. He had been abroad for six winters in succession, including four trips to Australia. He had played in fifty-nine Test Matches.

All that time he had been the team's key player, relied on to bowl for long spells, bat at Number 6, and field in the slips. He was also unfit. An old back injury troubled him and he had strained his left side.

The 1983 season was another struggle to find form. Botham did little of note in the World Cup or in the early Tests against New Zealand. But at last, in the final match, he came good with a glorious century off only 99 balls.

He followed this up with another fine hundred when England went to New Zealand that winter. He and Derek Randall came together at the wicket when the team was in trouble at 115 for 5. The pair added a highly entertaining 232 runs, with Botham scoring exactly 100 of his runs in boundaries!

Soon, however, less pleasant news hit the headlines. The tour was soured by complaints from the New Zealanders about the noisy behaviour of English team members in their hotel. England lost the next Test and the series. Most of this was unfairly blamed on Ian Botham who seemed to be at the centre of every row. Then, when the party moved on to Pakistan, he made some tactless remarks about the country and annoyed a lot of people. With great relief, he flew home early because of a knee injury.

Botham tried to put all this behind him in the 1984 season. He had a new challenge, as captain of the Somerset team, and was determined to do well. Sadly, he produced few fireworks: there were no big scores and only 33 wickets.

To make matters worse, the West Indies were once

again on tour. This time they beat England five times in a row — the most wretched defeat in her history. Botham fought hard with the bat, making three fifties, but his bowling was very expensive, except for a fine performance at Lord's when he took 8 for 103 in the first innings. But elsewhere he bowled too short, and seemed to have lost his knack of swinging the ball. Once again, he had failed to make his mark against the best team in the world.

9   Six-Hitter Supreme

When the England players set off for India in the winter of 1984, Ian Botham was not with them. He had decided to take a complete break from cricket and spend Christmas at home for a change. He also hoped for a break from the newspaper headlines.

However, Botham is not a man to sit still for long. Instead of cricket, he turned back to his second love — football. He trained with Scunthorpe United, and then, back in Somerset, he played for Yeovil Town. At his first home game, the club had the largest crowd in its history.

His fun on the football field was soon overshadowed by a new scandal. On New Year's Eve the police suddenly arrived at his home in Lincolnshire. After a search, they found a small amount of the drug cannabis. Botham protested that it was not his, but he was still taken to court and fined for possessing it illegally.

It was a cheerless beginning to the year. Once more, he was being sneered at in the newspapers for setting a bad example to young people. Some writers even began to suggest that the England team was better off without him. After all, hadn't they just played superbly to defeat the Indians? Was Botham really needed?

He swiftly proved the journalists wrong, by playing a series of dazzling innings for Somerset. Against Nottinghamshire, he hit 90 off only 77 balls. Against Glamorgan, he hit a century off 76 balls. The next opponents were the touring Australians, Botham's favourite enemies. He battered them for fifty in a mere 30 balls. A fortnight later, he scored an even more brilliant 149 against Hampshire, with six sixes and twenty fours.

After this explosive start, there was no way he could be left out of the Test side. In the first match of the series against Australia he took 7 wickets, held 2 blinding catches and scored 60 runs to help England to an easy win. After that, there was no more argument about leaving him out.

In the six Tests that summer he took 31 wickets — more than anyone else on either side. His batting was scarcely needed, as team-mates Robinson, Gower and Gatting piled up the runs. At Birmingham, for example, they all scored centuries against the inexperienced Australian bowlers. When Botham walked to the crease, the scoreboard read 572 for 4. What could he do to make his mark? The answer was simple. He hit his very first ball for a massive six.

For Somerset, too, he continued his six-hitting ways. Altogether he sent eighty sixes soaring over boundaries up and down the country. No-one had ever hit so many in an English season. He also scored three more centuries and finished with an average of 69 — the best of his career.

Unfortunately, Somerset did not share in his success.

Another wicket falls to Botham in the 4th Test against
Australia at Old Trafford

They won only one game and ended up bottom of the
County Championship table. The truth was that Botham
was not a good captain. He would set off, like a knight
in armour, to demolish the opposition and hope that
his team would follow him. But most of them couldn't.

Many of the young players became depressed at their
failures, and Botham found it difficult to talk to them.
He was often away from the county playing for
England. This left him tired and anxious to escape

from the glare of publicity. It was no surprise when he was replaced as captain by his long-time colleague Peter Roebuck at the end of 1985.

This was a real wrench for Botham, who hates giving up any challenge. But he had already begun to plan for another, and even tougher one. After a brief family holiday he set out to walk the length of England and Scotland from John O'Groats to Land's End.

A few months before, he had paid a visit to a special children's unit in a hospital in Taunton. There he had met many children suffering from leukaemia, a disease of the blood. 'They seemed as normal and happy as my own kids,' he said. 'But I was told many of them would

Botham chatting to a policeman on his famous charity walk
from John O'Groats to Land's End

soon be dead. It was shattering.' He was determined to raise money for research into this terrible illness, and a charity walk was a sensational way of doing it.

Botham and three faithful companions set out on 25 October. Along the way they were joined by scores of people, many of them celebrities such as the boxer John Conteh, and comedians Max Boyce and Billy Connolly. In every town and village on the route, crowds gathered to give money to the cause.

On and on Botham marched, covering twenty or thirty miles each day. He took only a short break to go to Doncaster Infirmary, where Kathryn had just given birth to their third child, Rebecca. At last, on 29 November, he reached Land's End, where he dressed up in top hat and tails and jumped into the sea!

'Botham's Walk' had been an astonishing success. He had covered 874 miles (1406 kilometres) in five weeks and raised £710,000 for charity. Once more he was a national hero. As he said later, 'It is the best thing I have done in my life.'

1985 had been a sensational year for Ian Botham. He had helped England win back the Ashes, set a new six-hitting record and made an heroic journey.

10 A New Start

Ian Botham's Test Match career has been a series of ups and downs. After his dramatic start in 1977 he shot to stardom. Then he became captain of England and his cricket suffered badly. After the enthralling summer of 1981 he was a superhero once more. Next, he had a string of failures, followed by yet another triumph over the Australians in 1985. Whatever was going to happen next?

Next, unfortunately, were the West Indians. The England team travelled out to the Caribbean full of confidence. They had just won two Test series and their major batsmen were scoring heavily. Botham was back in form. Surely they were not going to be humiliated this time.

But they were. The West Indian battery of opening bowlers sent down a barrage of terrifying bouncers and pounded England to defeat five more times. Not one English batsman scored a century. Botham himself had a worse time than ever. He failed to reach fifty and bowled very badly, taking only 11 wickets. This left him poised one wicket behind the world record set by Dennis Lillee.

Worst of all, he was hounded by newspaper reporters

wherever he appeared. Fast bowlers on the pitch and nosy journalists off it! He spent much of the tour in the privacy of his hotel bedrooms, frustrated and unhappy.

It was a wretched trip and everyone was pleased to get home for a short rest before the 1986 English season began. For Botham, however, a rest was out of the question. He was still being pursued by the journalists, who were desperately looking for a new scandal.

He soon provided them with one. In May 1986 he wrote a newspaper article in which he confessed that he had smoked the drug cannabis. He had always denied this before. The cricket authorities were horrified and banned him from playing in all matches for Somerset and England for two months.

Once again Botham's career was at rock bottom. Not only was he out of the Test side, but he couldn't play for Somerset either. The weeks seemed to drag by. In their Test Matches against India and New Zealand, the England team performed more badly than ever. Without Botham, they looked dull and uninspiring.

At last, in August, the ban came to an end and he was back. But did he deserve to go straight into the Test side? Crowds flocked eagerly to Weston-super-Mare to see what he would do in his come-back innings for Somerset. He rewarded them with a blistering display, scoring a hundred in an hour off only 66 balls.

Yet again he had proved that he was the most exciting batsman in England. He simply could not be ignored. And so he was selected for the very last Test Match of the summer, against the New Zealanders at the Oval.

The spectators held their breath as Botham ran in to

bowl his first ball. It was not a particularly good delivery, but the batsman Bruce Edgar edged the ball into the slips where Graham Gooch caught it. Botham took two more wickets in the innings. He now had 357 Test victims under his belt and was past Lillee's record. When his turn came to bat, he raced to a glorious fifty before a rainstorm ended the fun.

The season finished with another sort of storm. Somerset announced that they were sacking their two West Indian stars Viv Richards and Joel Garner. Botham was outraged. Immediately he promised that he too would leave the county if the pair were not kept on. Richards and Garner were two of his closest friends, and he felt he had to stand up for them.

While all this was boiling up, the England team set off on their next tour, an exhausting trip to Australia. Battered and despondent, they were now seen as having no hope against the Australians. It was quite a change from the start of their Caribbean journey at the beginning of the year.

In the First Test Match in Brisbane the tourists were struggling when their fourth wicket fell at 198. In marched Botham, determined to make his mark. Quietly at first, and then pasting the bowlers, he scored 138, his fourteenth Test century. Australia never recovered from this battering, and lost by 7 wickets.

England won the Fourth Test as well, after Botham and Gladstone Small had taken 5 wickets each to dismiss the home side for 141. So they had kept the Ashes — and Botham had once again played a vital part.

He enjoyed himself very much on the tour. Mike

Gatting, the new skipper, was a man he could respect and obey. Ian worked hard in the nets for him and bowled where he was told. There was a discipline to Botham's cricket which had not been seen for several years.

During the winter, Ian made two important announcements. One was that he was leaving Somerset, the club where he had spent his cricketing life, to join Worcestershire. The second was that he would not go on tour again for at least three years. Instead, he would spend his winters in Australia, playing for the state of Queensland.

Nobody was really surprised. He could not stay with Somerset after the sacking of Richards and Garner. A start with a different county might be refreshing for him. Likewise, the break from touring would give him time to relax. Instead of living in hotels, he would be able to buy a home in Australia and spend more time with his growing family.

As things turned out, his first season with Worcestershire in 1987 was not a great success, although he did help them win the Refuge Assurance Sunday League with some explosive batting. He also scored his first century with the team against Somerset, as he had promised to do. However, he did little else that was spectacular and missed several matches through injury.

England's Test series that summer against Pakistan was a disaster. Ruined by rain, it resulted in a victory for Pakistan, their first in England. Botham had a poor time with bat and ball, taking only a paltry 7 wickets. At the Oval, he was hit for no fewer than 217 runs — a

A spectacular batsman

record he would rather forget.

However, he continued to spring surprises. On the last day of that match, England were on the brink of defeat at 139 for 4. They were still more than 300 runs behind the Pakistanis. Botham came in to join his captain Gatting — and stayed for four-and-a-half hours. Pushing forward in defence and rarely risking an attacking shot, he played the most restrained innings of his life scoring only 51. It seemed that he really had made a new start.

Ian Botham has now been playing Test cricket for more than ten years. Without doubt, he is one of the greatest cricketers in the history of English cricket. But he is tired of the constant travelling and of the publicity which surrounds him. Perhaps three winters in Queensland will give him the break he so badly needs. You can be sure that there are more heroic performances to come from him yet.

Important Dates in Ian Botham's Career

2 September 1973	First match for Somerset first team, against Sussex in the Sunday League at Hove
12 June 1974	Scores heroic 45 not out in a Benson & Hedges game against Hampshire at Taunton
28 July 1977	First Test Match, against Australia at Nottingham
24 February 1978	First Test century — 103 against New Zealand at Christchurch
30 August 1979	Reaches the Test 'double' — 100 wickets and 1000 runs — in the Final Test against India at the Oval
18 May 1980	Appointed captain of England
7 July 1981	Resigns the captaincy
20 July 1981	Scores 140 not out against Australia at Leeds
8/9 July 1982	Highest Test score — 208 against India at the Oval
August 1984	Declines to go on England tour of India and spends the winter at home
10 August 1985	Hits his 67th six of the season against Northamptonshire at Weston-super-Mare to create a new record
21 August 1986	Breaks the record for number of Test wickets when taking his 356th against New Zealand at the Oval
25 April 1987	Begins the new season with a new county — Worcestershire
10 August 1987	Scores his 5000th run in Test cricket, against Pakistan at the Oval

Outstanding Achievements

Ian Botham has scored 5057 runs, taken 373 wickets and caught 109 catches in Test cricket — an all-round performance without parallel.

His highest score in first-class cricket is 228, against Gloucestershire at Taunton.

His fastest century was made in forty-nine minutes against Warwickshire at Birmingham in 1985.

In the Jubilee Test against India at Bombay in 1980, he scored 114 runs and took 13 wickets — the most remarkable match 'double' of all time.

He has scored a Test hundred and taken 5 wickets in an innings in the same match five times — also a record: 103 and 5 for 73 against New Zealand, 108 and 8 for 34 against Pakistan in 1978, 114 and 7 for 48 against India in 1980, 149 not out and 6 for 95 against Australia in 1981, and 138 and 5 for 59 against New Zealand in 1984.

His 118 against Australia at Old Trafford in 1981 was scored off only 102 balls, and he reached his 100 off only 86, making it one of the fastest Test centuries of all. He also hit six sixes — a record for Anglo-Australian matches.

He has scored fourteen Test centuries, and taken 5 wickets in an innings twenty-seven times during his 94 Test Matches.

During the 1981 Test series against Australia, he was named 'Man of the Match' in three games in a row.